FREE RANGE RISHI
THE SECRET CODE
TO HAPPINESS

JOURNEY TO THE HEART OF YOGA

CYRIL JOSEPH NEICHERIL

ISBN-9798682290109

Library of Congress Control Number: 2018675309
Printed in the United States of America

I dedicate this book to my wife Nikki, the love and support of my life. Your brilliant mind and companionship is much appreciated.

CONTENTS

INTRODUCTION

In writing this book, I hope to provide inspiration to those who seek the truth. The illuminating vision of the Rishis or Seers of realty is quite profound. Yoga is not a bunch of exercises. It is the science of mind. For thousands of years ancient Rishis dived into the depths of consciousness and came forth with a code of living that brings peace of mind. In the pages of this book you will find an inner roadmap to contentment.

How would you like to live a happier, less stressful, and worry-free life?

I wrote this book after a 58-year journey to help you achieve this state.

It is the culmination of living experiences that took me through four continents, highs and lows of corporate experience, and psychedelic states.

The Covid-19 Pandemic has uncovered that the life we hold as real and important can be wiped out in an instant. Jobs, businesses, relationships, and the self-image we project are not permanent. However, our attachment to our social identity creates suffering when it changes. This book is an in-depth transformational playbook to help you be centered, easeful, and peaceful no matter what you are faced with in life. The information is based on scholarly research and personal experience. It will reveal an approach to life rooted in the way of the Rishi. Enlightened beings from another age, Rishi means seer of reality.

We are all born into a social fabric that teaches us how to think. This is the beginning of sheep thinking and control of our minds. The root cause of suffering is brainwashed thinking. Taking what is impermanent as permanent and imagining what is not real as real is ignorance and the cause of pain. Modern society is full of marketed images we think of as desirable, controlled by powerful institutions. This controls our self-worth and therefore our minds.

What if I were to suggest your interpretation of life is a holographic reality created by your mind. In and of itself, it has no meaning other than what we as individuals ascribe to it. However, we make it real by attaching emotions and feelings to certain ideas, concepts, and people which manifests as real in our perspective. This is mostly due to our individual Karmic impulse and social conditioning.

We are taught by our parents, culture, and our early experiences as children what is important. For example, if you were taught being a rich person with a big house and expensive cars is desirable and can make you happy that becomes your reality. So, you spend many years studying, working, sacrificing, and playing hypocritical politics and get all you thought would make you happy. Then you succeed and find you are happy for a short time. However, you have to maintain this image and work like hell. You may feel stressed and less healthy than you want to be with blood pressure problems and a big gut. Nevertheless, you can now afford a big house and everyone on social media and in your family think you made it to the big time. However, you now have to live with the fear of losing it all, and find your behaviors and actions are guided by your possessions which now own you. Control through the accumulation of wealth is an illusion. We are born with nothing and leave with nothing.

Jesus pointed out, "It is easier for a camel to pass through the eye of a needle than for a rich man enter the kingdom of heaven".

This is not to say pursuing wealth is bad. No, it is a good thing if indeed you are balanced and happy and can manage your life despite the demands of sustaining someone else's image of success. My point is we create an image. In large part, the image rarely makes us internally happy. This is also why many marriages have trouble.

Many people marry an image not the real person. Coming to terms with the real person who has all sorts of emotions and feelings not the image creates tension. This takes emotional work. Many are unwilling or unable to confront and work through dysfunctional behavior and would rather get divorced or live a superficial life and project an image that is not sustainable. Note the rise of social media platforms and people pretending to have a life that is not based in reality. My experience has been excessive posts on such platforms are an effort to gain approval and recognition of others so people can validate their being. I have noted some people who seem to have fantastic lives posted and marketed by images of fun and glamor are actually quite bland in person. It all seems like one big popularity contest. This then gives insecure people FOMO "fear of missing out."

Being happy is aligning yourself with conscious energy, by supporting yourself in a comfortable manner, and maintaining a healthy body through regular exercise, good diet, and a balanced mind that is at peace. This does not require a materially focused life which is ever changing due to outward conditions. But a balanced centered one. This is what the Rishis taught. Keep things simple and focus on the non-changing inner vision which is peaceful, confident and radiant, and not bound to external possessiveness.

The Global Pandemic has made it transparent all that we thought was secure can be snatched away in an instant, by forces outside our control like an invisible virus. The entire economy has been impacted showing that without demand there is no economy. Demand comes from us. The more we consume the more garbage and pollution we create. The more we desire and possess the more anxiety and worry we have of losing what we have accumulated. My wife and I learned the best experiences are free, like a hike-in nature. So, learn to live within your means and simplify your life by untangling from unnecessary material possessions, dependencies, and engagements. I did not suddenly come up with this perspective. I evolved my thinking over time.

BREAKING WITH TRADITION

I grew up in the Catholic tradition and found the teachings of Jesus amazing and sound, however at an early age I developed an aversion to priests and ritual. It seemed to me a cult controlled by a bunch of guys in robes who were not enlightened at all.

My family who are quite devout Catholics would have priests over to our house. I have to say I found them nice on the surface but mostly pompous and full of false piety. This led me to question how these guys can have a special channel to God, and have the power to listen to our guilty feelings and forgive sin through the confession ritual. I said to myself, I could contact God directly through my own prayers and ask for help by talking to him without them.

My dad always used to convince me that priests had been given special power because Jesus said to his disciple Peter, "you are the rock on which I will build my church." Although, this is what we are taught, there is no real evidence this took place except for translations that are suspect. It is in fact Saul of Tarsus, later known as Paul the Apostle, a man who never met Jesus but who claimed to have a vision of Jesus, that was the main evangelizer of Christianity at the grassroots level. The rest was the Roman state who used religion as a tool.

It is well known, the Roman ruler, Emperor Constantine made Christianity the official religion of Rome, and only one version of Jesus was allowed. Official church doctrine was established at the Council of Nicaea as Cannon Law. Constantine sponsored it, and directed who would participate. In fact, it was decided here that Jesus was the Son of God and divine, and not an exceptional human who achieved an internal state that made him one with the universal life force we call God. This was done so the Roman empire could control the minds of people using organized religion. Up to this time many manuscripts indicated Jesus was an exceptional man with a highly developed spiritual vision. A revolutionary Rabbi or teacher who spoke up against the existing religious and political order. The same group of authority figures that orchestrated his crucifixion.

As I matured, I spent time in Catholic schools and began to see that many priests were corrupt, and some were sexual predators molesting children and nuns which did not sit well. This has now been widely exposed, and the Catholic church has paid billions in lawsuits to victims, and had a Pope resign. I also noted Priests use their social position as authority figures to control the minds of people through fear of hell. The very idea that a religion can excommunicate you from its presence, and shun you for thinking independently and differently from Church rules, seemed fodder for the weak minded. The whole thing seemed absurd.

That being said the current Pope Francis is making progressive changes, but he is meeting resistance from within. It is also true that secular branches of the church, such as Catholic Charities and Catholic Relief Services, do a lot to help the needy. This is noteworthy.

I thought to myself, Jesus said, "I am the truth the way and the life" and showed a code of conduct to achieving the union he had with the universal father. The statement he made "seek first the kingdom of heaven and all else will be added on to you" stuck with me. As did the Our Father prayer. It clearly is a prayer seeking alignment with God through faith.

As I evolved, I also began to be aware everyone was seeking status and power, so they could be superior or get everyone's approval for their self-image. Race and culture also seemed to be a big deal, with white people dominating authority positions and defining the scope of opportunity available to people of color. I also noted that men-controlled women with role definitions.

I myself belong to a clan of landowning high-born Indians, from Kerala state in India known as Knanaya, who trace their origins to the Middle East and follow an Eastern Orthodox style of Christianity. They trace their origins from Thomas of Cana, a Middle Eastern merchant who settled in Kerala's Malabar coast with 72 Christian families around 350 CE. The King of Kerala welcomed them and gave them special privileges and rights including land and the right to build churches. This became the fountain head of Christianity in South Kerala. Even though they are a small minority in Kerala, they own large tracts of land, businesses, and are influential in politics.

Many Knanaya people including my family immigrated to the United States in the 1970-1980 timeframe. Houston, Tx and Chicago, IL both have large groups who have been established for two generations. They are a highly educated group of immigrants, mostly successful people in the medical sciences, education, and engineering fields. They, like several immigrant groups, are tribal and practice endogamy, meaning only marry within the tribe and are closed minded to outsiders.

I was fortunate that my parents were educators. We traveled and lived in East Africa, Central Africa, Asia, and finally settled in America. I guess, I was always at the intersection of religion, culture, and race. This gave me a broad perspective. It seemed culture and tribalism went hand in hand. The age of Donald Trump has clearly demonstrated tribal sentiments run deep. People are very reluctant to accept change from their group culture and identity, even in a great nation like America that promotes freedom, diversity, and individuality. This is the same in all countries, all one needs to do is observe world cup soccer or American football. Tribal roots are so rampant, people often get rabid and violent in support of the team they support. This herd mentality is quite prevalent. Because of this, people separate themselves from each other and do not see the interconnectedness we all have. The truth is we are all animated by the same energy that is flowing through matter. We have more similarities than differences.

I think from the very onset, I was wired not to fit in. Having had a multicultural upbringing and experience, my vision was more inclusive and not based on us and them thinking. My parents always provided me with a comfortable environment where I could express my views, even though I must have been a real pain in the ass by challenging their beliefs.

EVOLUTION OF THINKING

At the age of 8, I experienced an out of body experience that both frightened and inspired me. I woke up to find myself staring at my sleeping body from the ceiling of my room. I became scared and the moment I did I returned to my body. I told my Mom, but she was skeptical. Several weeks later I experienced the same thing, only this time my awareness began to fly over the land. I saw animals and people before I returned to my body again. I kept quiet because I felt no one would believe me. This experience taught me to think a little differently. I never experienced this phenomenon again. However, I became open minded to other schools of thought. How could it be that I was disembodied but alive! I began to sense there was more to existence than what we are taught.

I decided that I would only believe what I personally experienced and validate that experience with ancient scriptures and critical thinking. By 12, I had mastered Bible studies. My parents were very devout and the family would collectively kneel and recite the Rosary before dinner. This practice established that I needed to surrender my ego to a higher power. The Christian values I grew up with also taught me tolerance and self-discipline.

What I found interesting is I never classified people by race, religion or anything like that. I addressed people from a very young age as energy. If someone was nice to me, I saw no barriers to communication and interaction. As I grew up, I found this was not the case with everyone. Most people were bound by their culture, race, and upbringing, and were biased against others who were different from them. This, I observed, was prevalent in institutional environments and with authority figures and gatekeepers, such as hiring staff, police, even hostesses in restaurants where many people who are different are often marginalized by the way they are treated. These days it is mostly unconscious bias, but it exists.

The unnecessary brutality in the treatment of black men by police has uncovered systemic racist behavior is prevalent in society. Nationwide protests and the toppling of confederate symbols are demonstrating anger. Most reasonable people realize there is a problem and something needs to be done about it.

Though physical differences amongst people exist on a superficial level, they occurred due to environmental and cultural reasons. As humans 99% of our DNA is similar.

THE ORDEAL OF LEARNING AND UNDERSTANDING THE MATRIX

As I became a man, I pursued a degree in Political science and completed graduate studies in Communication and Health Behavior; later moving into Personal Training and Life Coaching.

While in college I was a good student and involved in boxing but a bit of a party animal. One day while partying with some fellow students, Vladimir and Sergei at the University of Houston, I experimented with LSD. While tripping, I observed my friend Nikki who I would eventually marry glowing with a bright shine I had never seen, though everyone else around her seemed to be decaying. Orbs of white light were all around her. LSD lets you see other dimensions of reality. A well-known mental state narrated by Steve Jobs, founder of Apple. I knew somehow my life would be better off with her in it, and pursued her for one year till she accepted me. She was an athlete and did not want me indulging in any substance other than endorphins produced by exercise and the buzz of fine wine. So that was that with the excessive indulgence. We ended up taking weight training and Yoga classes together and hooked up. She later became a national class marathoner and successful person in the corporate world.

After I met my future wife things began to settle. In 1984, I came across the writings of a man called Adi Da Samraj, previously known as Franklin Jones, who wrote books on how the ego was a contraction from the true self. He was a westerner and not from the Indian tradition. He studied Yoga in India and had some interesting books, like Easy Death. Elizabeth Kubler Ross, a pioneer expert on the stages of death and dying, noted this book as a seminal body of work. He narrated the complicated Vedic Sanskrit teaching for the Western mind to grasp. I later discovered he was trained by Swami Muktananda, a famous Indian mystic who practiced Siddha Yoga.

Adi Da struggled with his human impulses and pursuit of the divine, swinging from excess to austerity. He had to move to Fiji, due to some scandals around sex and women, where he continued to have a large following till, he died. Nevertheless, his work influenced me as I was in the same state of pursuing spirituality as well as sense pleasures. He postulated the concept of ego contraction from the real self as the cause of much misery and applied it to his teachings. In essence, we contract away from connected relationships with other people due to our ego.

During this time, I was also drawn towards Native American Shamanism whose emphasis is respecting father sky and mother earth, and the wisdom of using sound and plants for healing. Native Americans were foremost in connecting with and respecting nature and living in harmony with it. Shamans connected the spiritual world with the material through a perspective. I met some Shamans who belonged to the Native American Indian church. They taught me that we live in a multiverse. A vision must be sought to live in it.

I learned through them, If I was able to shift my perception then I would see things differently. I participated in a Peyote ceremony where a drink is made from a cactus and passed around, along with chanting and beating of a deer skin drum, in the presence of a firepit. The wisdom of The Great Spirit is invoked for guidance. The Peyote has a hallucinogenic effect. What I experienced was that my life was a kaleidoscope that was shaped by how I viewed things. I had the power to shift my perception like changing the adjustment of a kaleidoscope, and thus the configuration and my interpretation of life could shift. This is the skill a Shaman uses in working with patients. Shifting a person's perspective to make them feel better.

In college, I took a course in Western Philosophy and found the teachings of Pythagoras interesting. Most people recognize him because of Pythagoras theorem and his contributions to geometry. However, very few know he studied in Asia and Egypt, believed in the concept of reincarnation, astrology, and being kind to animals. He recognized their spirit was identical to ours though their bodies are different. In fact, it is documented, he could communicate with animals and was a strict vegetarian. His teachings emphasized the immortality and reincarnation of the soul, virtuous and humane behavior toward all living things, and the concept of geometric mathematics. He advocated a clear mind and logical thinking for an objective comprehension of reality.

I later got caught up with my own changing life and urges, and left my spiritual quest behind for several years. Nevertheless, I always was drawn to books on spiritual wisdom and continued to read.

We moved from Houston to Portland, OR. I attended graduate school, had a career as a Seminar Leader, Market Research Director, and OSHA Instructor before shifting into Personal Training and Life Coaching. I had a health crisis requiring three surgeries and returned to my Spiritual quest.

In 2000, I got Certified as an Ayurvedic Health Educator, and several years later in Vedic Astrology from The American Institute of Vedic Studies. David Frawley also known as Pandit Vamadeva Shastri is the Founder. He is the author of many great books on Eastern Metaphysics and an expert in Yoga, Ayurveda, and Vedic Astrology. This gave me a structured foundational knowledge of both subjects. I went on to advance my studies on my own.

I started a website called Ancienthealer.com selling Ayurvedic herbs and providing basic advice on the benefits of an Ayurvedic lifestyle. I was successful and had clients from as far away as Brazil and Italy. However, I was not ready to advance spiritually. I later shut the site down and pursued a job as a Market Research

Director where I was offered three times what I was making with my website. I resumed a material lifestyle chasing money, booze, good steak, and status and forgot about spirituality again for several years. I was not really happy; however, I satisfied my needs for short term gratification and the need for money.

Seeking answers to my life which was not bad but unfulfilling, I experimented with meditation, consulted astrologers and got readings in both Western and Vedic astrology.

I was more drawn to Vedic astrology which I became acquainted with in my Ayurveda learnings, as it had a scientific basis and is more ancient.

Intrigued by Jyotish, or the Science of light, which is the original term for Vedic astrology, I began to study and learn more about it. After consulting with several Vedic Astrologers and not being satisfied, because they seemed to be vague and esoteric, I got a reading and some advice from one of the greatest Vedic astrologers in America, a guy called Chakrapani Ulalal. He motivated me to study the science and explained my obsession with spirituality would not end till I mastered Spirituality, on account of Rahu being in my 9th house and Moon in my ascendant. Over the next several years I read everything I could get my hands on in Vedic Science.

I realized that Vedic astrology was just a tool to give higher insights and part of integrative Yoga. This brought me to the works of Swami Satchidananda Saraswathi. He was a great Yogi who was a student of one of the greatest Masters of Yoga India has ever known, Swami Sivananda of Rishikesh, founder of the Divine Life Society. Satchidananda was present in the opening ceremony at Woodstock and made a great comment that "America has progressed greatly in the material field, but it is time to progress in the Spiritual field."

The main practices of Integral Yoga focus on restoring the ease and peace of body and mind. Swami Satchidananda defined "disease" as the disturbance of one's natural ease which is the cause of disease. Prevention of mental agitation and restoration of equanimity are the hallmarks of Integral Yoga practices. He was also a big fan of the Bagavad Gita.

Seeking deeper answers, I went to South India the birthplace of my parents. Since I was an American not born in the land of my ethnicity, I decided to do a pilgrimage of sorts with my mom and dad. They took me to many temples, like the Meenakshi temple in Madurai, Sri Pandnamaswami temple in Trivandrum, Mahadeva Shiva Temple in Ettumanur, Vivekananda rock temple in Kanyakumari, and finally the ashram of Adi Shankaracharya, Kerala's own spiritual master, located in in Kaladi near Cochin. I thank my parents for indulging me and sponsoring the trip, particularly my mother who took care of all the travel details.

 Adi Shankara reformed the corruption that had affected Vedantic teachings and returned it to the spiritual origins through debate and self-inquiry. He compiled a refresh of The Upanishads or Forest Wisdom of Old. Just like the Catholic church, the Hindu faith had been taken over by corrupt abusive Brahmin priests in medieval times who used ritual and false idols to control the masses and manipulate their minds.

 Adi Shankara propagated a summation of Vedic thought that Moksha or freedom from suffering can be attained in this lifetime through self-effort. There is one underlying unity to all life that never changes and is the seed of all life. He put forth the perspective that through self-effort and self-analysis we can transcend the metal construct we are taught to believe is real. This philosophy is called Advaita Vedanta. I liked him because of his analytical mindset and critical thinking.

It was at his ashram; I made a commitment to meditate and study ancient knowledge that would lead to a happier life. It was here I got a copy of his book "The Crest Crown Jewel of Intellectual Discrimination." In the book, he explains Advaita Vedanta, an understanding of the theory of unity, and that Moksha or Spiritual liberation is achievable while being alive. It is a state of being not a place to go. Simple living, critical thinking, and self-analysis are a key part.

He propagated the idea that all phenomenal reality was in fact an illusion called Maya. There is no meaning to anything other than what we ourselves attribute to things. It is all self-created drama that is a subset of society's drama.

A good example of Maya is how we define beauty and the popularization of a type of look. All beings are made up of the elements which manifest as, flesh, blood, and bone encased in skin. Nevertheless, we get absorbed by what we are conditioned to be attracted to. Fashion magazines historically have expressed an ideal of beauty which we are then brainwashed to accept. This is then monetized through advertising.

Many women have developed self-esteem problems trying to be thin, pale and expressionless which is sold as the ideal of beauty through the fashion merchandizing and cosmetic industry. Society has now acknowledged this is a narrow definition, and things are changing to accept the diversity of beauty, but we have a long way to go. We now know many of the models till recently suffered from eating disorders to meet the ideal.

Another idea that is propagated that light skin is more attractive than dark skin which has led to the self-hatred of many dark-skinned people. Check out the skin bleaching and skin lightening industry, particularly in the southern hemisphere, plus people bleaching their hair and wearing contact lenses to change the color of their eyes.

Of course, beauty is in the eye of the beholder. Personally, as a straight male, I always found healthy, athletic, powerful, animated women with a clear complexion, regardless of race or color, attractive which is why I married a Persian lady with those traits.

A good example of how our minds are controlled is how the media distorts facts to control the emotions of people. All you need to do is watch FOX news, which is right leaning in its presentation, and then CNN which is left wing. Each channel focuses on its audience and distorts the facts to agitate the feelings of people and sell advertising. Somewhere in there is a kernel of truth.

When you simplify your life, live within your means, think independently, and seek your own acceptance, not chasing the approval of others, it brings liberation. Disciplining your mind to think straight and seek the truth from what you personally experience aligns you with cosmic energy which is flowing by its own potency.

I found that through meditation and living a life of simplicity, I was able to observe my thoughts and see where they were originating from. This eased my anxiety, as I realized I was the creator of my thoughts. This is a vital skill in understanding the way of the ancient Rishis. Most of us get caught up in our own self-created dramas by attaching our feelings to our thoughts. This results in getting caught up. I began to conceptually understand all thought originates from a vast intelligent field of Consciousness. We superimpose meaning and attributes which creates feelings and reactions. Contentment is a choice.

The secret to being happy is taking 100% responsibility for your own emotional wellbeing, by connecting with the source of all despite your material circumstances caused by Karma. This is Yoga. This is not easy and that is why I am writing this book.

There is no need of a priest, or anyone else for that matter. Neither is there a need to wear orange clothes and be a beggar to achieve inner peace. Only you can connect with the almighty through self- discipline and a shift in awareness. This is called Self- realization. The way of the Rishi is connecting with inner cosmic forces, releasing one from much earthly suffering, by entering a perception that transcends mundane attachments and expectations.

Life is indeed a progression of time with many events that happen along the way. It is up to us to align with cosmic energy and transcend the changes. As Jim Morrison, a great American Shaman and lead singer of The Doors once said, "No one gets out of here alive."

Every one of us is going to go through pain and loss. Fortunately, there is a roadmap that was developed by spiritually advanced beings called Rishis in Ancient times to surf the wave of pain.

FOUNDATIONS OF YOGA
AND THE SOLAR WAY

The Solar way is a 5000-year old, perhaps much older, code to living founded in India. Ancient India was filled with observers of the stars and enlightened kings. The epic Vedas, and later works like the Upanishads of enlightened Master Rishis or Seers, pointed out humans are non-binding modifications of an ultimate source of energy that is all pervading, ever expanding, and is the cause of all matter.

The visible form of divine energy is the Sun. The Sun is the visible form of Consciousness supporting all life through its rays. Like Egypt and the Aztecs in South America, the Sun was worshiped in India. Living in harmony with the seasons which are related to the Sun and Moon was the priority.

This is the basis of connecting with higher Consciousness. This is the ancient practice taught by the ancient Rishis. This is Universal law.

This ultimate reality is a state of enduring pure bliss Consciousness which can be tuned into by self-effort, through Yoga and meditation. It is the source of energy in a seed that produces a tree, or in an egg and sperm that creates a being. I will reveal an ancient code to achieving a state of being where you are easeful, peaceful, content, and not reliant on anyone else for your well-being.

Of course, we need a roof over our head, food, companionship of our family and good health. Apart from that, we attach too much importance to things. Fear of losing one's concept of oneself is what creates fear and anxiety. It is key to have a perspective freeing one from stress and anxiety.

 Maharishi Patanjali the author of the Yoga Sutras postulated "The restraint of the modification of the mind stuff is Yoga. Then the Seer abides in its own nature."

Maharishi Patanjali laid out in simple to understand terms a specific approach to achieve peace of mind. His ideas are a distillation of the teachings of Vedic thought. I urge anyone to read a copy of the Yoga Sutras, as it is simple to comprehend. Mental equilibrium is the goal of Yoga.

 However, the mind is unstable, capricious, jumps around like a monkey and seeks many things. Thoughts come like waves crashing onto rocks. One can have wealth but still remain unhappy and fearful.

The Rishis noted that the movement of the planets and their position in space affected physical life on earth and influenced our mind and emotional state. The thought waves and ingrained behavior patterns in our minds are known as Samskaras. This is Karma. These Samskaras, or impulses, manifest as the inner personality attracting external circumstances. Depending on our individual response or reaction, the outcomes can be positive or negative. Transcending fear, anger, and possessiveness can have a big impact on the quality and circumstances of life.

THE SCIENCE OF VEDIC ASTROLOGY

T he ancient Rishis were observers of the stars. Over thousands of years the relationship between man and the cosmos was understood by them. There are seven planets that affect life on earth and two nodes of the Moon that cause eclipses of the Sun and the Moon, for a total of nine planets, known as Navagraha. Nava is nine and Graha means to grip. These nine points of planetary energy have the power to grasp and influence human life.
The Rishis viewed the planets as transmission stations for interstellar energy. How they got this information is a mystery, since no advanced telescopes or knowledge of electromagnetism would have existed in ancient times.

Nevertheless, it appears the Rishis had advanced knowledge of astronomy and mathematics. The seven planets and two elliptical points or Navagraha are the Sun, Moon, Mercury, Venus, Mars, Jupiter, Saturn and the north and south nodes of the Moon, known as Rahu and Ketu which are electromagnetic points but are given the status of planets due to their powerful influence. Neptune and Pluto are not considered in Vedic Astrology. Physics tells us the solar system was created by a cloud of interstellar gas that collapsed under its own gravity and created the Sun. The particles around it became the planets due to gravitational and magnetic cosmic forces. The earth is one of those planets. Our bodies are made of the earth elements. Therefore, planetary influences affect our bodies as we are star-stuff imbued by universal

Consciousness. The movement of the earth in relation to planets affects us physically and mentally at an astral level.

Vedic Astrology is distinctly different from what we think of as astrology here in the West. The difference is that in Vedic Astrology we use the sidereal zodiac. Sidereal zodiac is based on the fixed observable positions of the constellations, as we see them in the sky. Western astrology, in contrast, uses what is called the tropical zodiac. The tropical zodiac is based not on the fixed observable positions, but rather on the relative and change-able position of the Sun which is a mathematical point that starts on the Sun's location on the Vernal equinox.

In Vedic Astrology, we don't think of people in terms of their Sun sign, as we do in Western astrology. Instead, we enter the chart through what is called the "Ascendant" or Lagna, the constella-tion that is rising on the Eastern horizon at the time of a person's birth. This sets up the harmonic relationship between the planets at the time of birth, and gives clues about an individual's person-ality, physical body, and the way the person presents themselves to the world. In short, your Karmic blueprint.

The Moon is also important in Vedic astrology. The Moon spends approximately one day in each one of 27 lunar mansions, or as-terisms, known as Nakshatras. Vedic Astrology is more accurate and predictive. It uses a system known as the Vimshotra Dasha system which can show when certain events will take place based on the Birth Nakshatras or the placement of the Moon when you were born. This is also the basis of relationship compatibility, as the Moon is the mind and emotions. This gives a much more ac-curate interpretation of a life.

Each planet rules a period of time in our lives known as a Maha Dasha or Great Period. A second planet will also be color-ing events known as an Antra Dasha. The position of these two planets on the birth chart, what they represent, and where they are placed, indicates the areas of life that will be activated at any given time.

Maharishi Parashara states "The unborn Lord has many incarnations. He has incarnated, as the nine (Nava) Graha to bestow on the living beings the results due to their Karmas. He is Janardan. He assumed the auspicious form of Graha's to destroy the demons (evil forces) and sustain the divine beings (dharma)".

The Sun revolves around the Galactic center of the Milky Way every 230 million years. The earth revolves around the Sun every year, the moon around the earth every month. Jupiter takes 12 years and Saturn 29 years. Cycles within cycles. It is from the Sun that all planets were created, and it is from the Sun that life emanates from. Consider plants transform sunlight into food through photosynthesis. All the planets including the moon reflect the Sun's electromagnetic frequency and radiated light. All living beings depend on the Sun for life! Our body is a composition of the periodic table of elements which came from the earth which is a fragment of the Sun. Carbon, Hydrogen, Oxygen, Nitrogen, Calcium, Phosphorous, Magnesium make up 99% of the human body. The Sun has a Heliosphere or magnetic field that is carried by the solar wind and covers the entire planetary system. In other word, the Sun's magnetic field covers all the planets.

It is well known that the earth has an electromagnetic field that interacts with solar energy and protects us from the harmful effects of the Sun. The human body also has an electromagnetic field that operates on a cellular level. Take for instance an EKG that measures the heart's electrical field. When someone has a heart attack, the electric field around the heart is disrupted and a shock from a defibrillator is given to reset the rhythm of the heart.

On a cellular level, the human body has a cellular field with positive and negative ions. This rhythm is maintained by electrolytes: Sodium, Potassium, Magnesium and Calcium. These are positive and negative ions moving in our fluids. Our internal field interacts with the earth's field which interacts with the planetary field. We are part of a cosmic fabric. This is the science behind why planets can influence us.

According to the ancient science of Jyotish, or Vedic astrology, each incarnated soul comes with its own frequency. There are twelve constellations: Aries, Taurus, Gemini, Cancer, Leo, Virgo, Libra, Scorpio, Sagittarius, Capricorn, Aquarius, and Pieces. Each sign relates to one of four elements: Ether, Air, Water, Fire and Earth. Each sign has a ruling planet and color associated with it. Light travels from the Sun and is reflected into the color spectrum by the planets. VIBGYOR: Violet, Indigo, Blue, Green, Yellow, Orange and Red. Light is also reflected through the human mind and body.

At the moment of birth when the first breath is taken and the umbilical cord is cut independent life begins. At that precise moment, the sign on the eastern horizon where the sun rises determines the light frequency the body becomes energized with. This becomes the determining factor in how we express our life force.

The birth chart is divided into 360 degrees, divided into 12 x 30-degree sections, one for each sign. Each 30-degree section is a house that represents an aspect of life. The sign in the first house is your rising sign which represents the self. Each planet symbolizes different aspects of your life. The Sun your Soul, Moon how you interpret life emotionally, Mercury how you apply your rational mind and speech, Jupiter how you expand, Venus how you enjoy, Mars your vital force, Rahu the north node your obsession, Ketu your past. It is possible to analyze a birth chart and predict with a high degree of accuracy how a soul will manifest itself.

The Nakshatras provide an environment within which the planetary energy can express themselves. They are fixed stars. Each one has a presiding deity and meaning. The placement of Rahu and Ketu in Signs and Nakshatras is important as it triggers events. For example, Covid 19 developed when Rahu was in the air sign Gemini and Ardra Nakshatra, related to the storm god Rudra and its symbol a teardrop. Ketu was in the fire sign Sagittarius and Mula Nakshatra which represents the root of things and the goddess of destruction Nirriti. Every time historically this position has happened it represented great change through suffering for the people on earth! The last time a similar configuration occurred a nuclear bomb dropped on Japan.

It is outside the scope of this book to go into a detailed discussion on Vedic astrology, however, understanding the mechanics simplifies the understanding of how we are connected to greater being through our bodies. So where did this knowledge come from many thousands of years ago? Legend has it came from the sunken continent of Kumari Kundam.

TRANSCENDENTAL KNOWLEDGE
AND THE LOST CONTINENT
OF KUMARI KUNDAM

In the Bhagavad Gita, the mythical Sun god Surya was taught Yoga by Krishna in his original form as Supreme Consciousness. The Vishnu Purina points out Surya transmitted the science of Yoga to Manu the first man. He ruled a kingdom of Dravidians and came from Kumari Kundam, a land stretching from the south of India to Australia and as far as Madagascar. Some call it Lemuria. The Aboriginal people of Australia have similar genetics to some older indigenous tribes in South India who still populate some areas of Kerala and Tamil-Nadu and look quite similar. Plato and Aristotle also talk about Atlantis in their writings which existed in a different age before being submerged. Kumari Kundam, like Atlantis, is described in Tamil literature as a land of spiritually advanced thinking with the use of gems and crystals to harness energy from the Sun. Women were venerated in this land. The word Kumari is Virgin Princess.

After the Ice age ended around 12000-15000 years ago, Kumari Kundam similar to the legend of Atlantis, as described by the Greek philosophers, was submerged under the ocean. large parts of Dravidia, current day South India: Tamil Nadu, Karnataka, Andhra, Srilanka, and Kerala were also impacted by Tsunamis. This became the land of the Dravidian people who migrated from the submerged continent.

This is quite plausible. When the Ice age ended, it is well known that many land masses were submerged and subducted due to plate tectonics and glacial melt. Much of the previous land mass and civilizations disappeared under hundreds of meters of ocean and the crust of the earth. I myself traveled to Kania Kumari at the edge of South India. Below the water are visible man-made granite structures of a different time. The temple dedicated to virgin Goddess Kumari is over 3000 years old, and she is said to have come from the subducted land.

It is recorded in ancient scriptures, known as the Puranas written by Veda Vyas, like the story of Noah, there was a big flood. Manu moved his entourage along with seven Rishis, known as the Saptarishis, to the Indian subcontinent where one of his progenies, Ikshavaku, became the King of the Solar Dynasty. The spiritual knowledge that came with them made its way to the foothills of the Ghats Mountain range in the South and the Himalayas in the North. There is historical evidence to show as the glaciers began to melt at the end of the ice age, the sea levels rose, and the climate changed. This would cause lower areas to flood and lead to migration of people over time to higher ground.

King Rama, of the epic Ramayana, is one of Manu's descendants and a Solar King. Rishi Vasishta and Rishi Agastya were two of seven sages Manu brought from the old continent. Both were receptacles of Yogic knowledge from the ancient land. Rishi Agastya remained in the south and began the Tamil Sangam, Tamil language, and Siddha tradition in the South, in the city currently known as Madurai. Vasishta's influence was in the North where the Vedic culture flourished around the Saraswathi river till, it dried up 4000 years ago. Traditional historians postulated that the Vedic civilization came from Central Asia and Iran, and conquered an inferior people who populated the Indian Subcontinent.

  However, the migration of people, from the South to the North, and the intermixing of cultures to create the Vedic culture is a more plausible history. The Indo Aryan invasion of North India, and the Vedic civilization coming into the subcontinent from the

North which has been popularized is a political creation.

This Aryan invasion theory from the North by light skinned people with a superior culture and the subjugation of dark-skinned indigenous people was propagated by Max Muller, a Christian Indologist who was sponsored by the British East India Company in the 1800's. He was a great scholar but subject to his own European bias. He was supported in his efforts by Colonialist Lord Thomas Babington Macaulay who became the head of India's education system. He destroyed the Indian educational system and replaced it with a British system and interpretation of history. He replaced Sanskrit with English. He despised Indians and viewed Indian culture as inferior.

There is evidence the North was invaded by Central Asian tribes, Mongols, Persians, and Alexander the Great. These war like people had superior weapons made of bronze, horse driven chariots, and fire rituals. However, they merged with the existing spiritual belief system. The Dravidian culture was much older and existed for thousands of years before these invasions. The preexisting spiritual dimension was incorporated by the new invaders. The whole Caste system evolved at this time as a means of stratification to, maintain the dominance of the lighter skinned invaders.

While there are several lines of Rishis, Vasishta and Agastya were two of the most important foundational Rishis India experienced in the North and South.

It is this line of Rishis that brought the ancient science of Santana Dharma, or the eternal way, to the Indian subcontinent. In ancient times, India was called Bharath after King Bharath a decedent of Ikshavaku. This is the line of kings and sages who practiced Solar worship or eternal way, till it got lost due to foreign invasions.

The Persians and British later conquered India and called it the land of Hindu, a name that comes from The Sindhu river. The people following a code of living called the eternal way became labeled as Hindus and later as Indians. The people in the Indus valley practiced Yoga, Ayurveda, and Vedic astrology along with meditation and venerated the planets.

This knowledge of Yoga can be traced in large part to the Maharishi Vasishta who was the preceptor of the Solar Dynasty and teacher of King Rama.

Maharishi Vasishta's conversation with King Rama was recorded by Sage Valmiki, author of the Ramayana, and is known as Yoga Vasishta. It explains the essence of Yoga. It is a great book for advanced Yoga practitioners.

Tired with all the pleasures of life, Rama became despondent and sought Vasishta's advice. Vasishta taught Rama that it was normal for him to have become fed up with all the transitory experiences of material existence, and he should seek the reality of life through introspection. This is a similar story to Buddha but much older.

Vasishta explained to Rama, Consciousness exists in four states in a human being: waking, sleeping, dreaming, and Turya. This is the fourth state, a transcendental state of being where one can achieve a super conscious awareness also known as Moksha or freedom from illusion.

He pointed out all forms that exists are non-binding modifications of Consciousness experiencing itself in different formats. Vasishta's knowledge can be traced to subsequent generations.

Vasishta's progeny was Maharishi Parashara, founder of Vedic astrology, and author of The Brihat Parashara Hora Shastra which is the most comprehensive work in Vedic astrology. It took me one year to get through it and several more to understand it. Parashara fathered Veda Vyas, the author of The Vedas which are some of the oldest books in the world. The Rig Veda is the oldest of the Vedas and has complex hymns about Indra, Agni, Vayu, Soma, Suraya, Rudra, and Varuna. These are esoteric poems explaining cosmic forces of lightning, thunder, fire, wind, Moon, water, and Sun. Rudra was later associated with Shiva.

The code to understanding this is that all these elements are inside us and connect us to the cosmic being. The Rig Veda is written as poetry and has hidden esoteric meaning. The main thing to comprehend is we are interconnected with natural forces. Aligning ourselves with cosmic energy is the purpose of life.

I will bring forth the esoteric meanings of ancient Vedic science for practical application in a modern world. I will also unlock the Vedic code. The eternal way is essentially a respect for natural law. Santana Dharma.

Some of the important ancient Sages that showed the way and influenced my thinking were Sage Kapila and his Samkhya Philosophy; Maharishi Vasishta teacher of Rama; Veda Vyas author of The Rig Veda, Mahabharata, Bhagavad Gita, and Puranas. The Bhagavad Gita also known as the song of god is the essence of Yoga.

I gained additional insights from Upanishads or forest wisdom, Adi Shankara the reformer who restored the original teachings of the Upanishads. And of course, Jesus of Nazareth who I considered an enlightened being and an incarnation of God's word on the planet. The sermon on the mount is indeed a roadmap to inner wellbeing and cosmic connection to the Universal life force. Consider the statement "whatsoever you do to the least of my brothers you do on to me."

It is interesting to note, the birth of Jesus was heralded by three wise men from the east following a star. Is that not astrology? It is also recorded Joseph and Mary took Jesus to Egypt to escape Herod. Between the ages of 12 and 29, before he began preaching there is no record of him. Many scholars believe he went back east, traveled to Persia and India where the wise men came from, and where he studied. Upon his return he was baptized by John and began to teach. Due to the spiritual wisdom he propagated, his message of peace and love rings eternal.

Jesus' spiritual message was simple and outside the context of any organized mass religion. An inner vision and code of living to transcend earthly misery. This is identical to Santana Dharma.

THE ETERNAL WAY TO JOYFUL LIVING

Santana Dharma teaches value based principled living and how to balance your life. There are four areas: living a life of accountability and responsibility, pursuit of material prosperity, the enjoyment of the senses and the physical body, and spiritual self-realization.

Balancing and integrating these four areas of life is the art of living well. Then we experience a state of understanding that life is flowing by its own potency. Aligning oneself with conscious living while observing your tendencies is the key. This involves ten specific steps.

1. Align yourself with the super Consciousness. Life is experiencing you through your body and not the other way around. This is self-realization.
2. Self-discipline over your senses and meditation with conscious breathwork is key to relaxing your body and mind.
3. Practice truthfulness, non-violence, and simple living. This unclutters your life.
4. Respect all forms of human and animal life, by understanding unity in diversity. We are all a manifestation of the same energy.
5. Seek your own approval and do not idolize others who seem to have a better superficial life than you. Everyone has problems.
6. Respect your parents and give leeway to your elders for

they have seen more than you.
7. Cultivate fearlessness with compassion.
8. Observe and master: fear, anger, greed, possessiveness, and lust, for they will cause you unnecessary pain.
9. Practice critical thinking and see clearly what is appearing. Life is filled with illusion and those that peddle it.
10. Spend time in living nature for it puts us in touch with living energy and mother earth. Gardening is a great way of doing this if you live in a city.

UNLOCKING THE RISHI CODE

The Rishi code is a vison of life that is multidimensional and based on energetics. Some context to understanding and unlocking this code of thinking comes from Rishi Kapila. He is also mentioned in the Bhagavad Gita as the best of sages, and is the founder of Samkhya Philosophy. Buddha was born in Kapila Vaastu, a town founded on Sage Kapila's thinking. It is clear he was influenced by this thinking.

Sage Kapila taught existence has two elements: Purusha Consciousness and Prakriti matter. Prakriti consists of Rajas (movement, activity, change), Tamas (inertia, materiality, darkness) and Sattva (harmony, balance, intelligence). It is constantly changing between these states. Prakriti is creation and by its instability creates matter. It does this by drawing from the five elements, Ether, Air, Fire, Water, and Earth to create substance. This is what constitutes living matter.

Purusha is pure bliss Consciousness and activates Prakriti. The ego reflects Consciousness through matter, and separates us by focusing on external sense perception.

Sight, touch, sound, smell, and taste focus our awareness outside, creating an internal holographic reality. This leads to possessiveness, greed, lust and anger. I and mine clouds the mind and is the root cause of suffering. The truth is we came without possessions and we will leave with nothing except our experience. The Buddha pointed out all life is suffering and suffering comes from attachment.

In my view, the research indicates much of what the Buddha

taught was in existence far beyond his time. However, he had his own path and came from a royal family which gave him street cred, and popularized Buddhism as a Philosophy. It should be noted Buddha died as a mortal in his eighties. All his teachings are about a way of thinking, a mental state of mind, and an approach to life in order to escape the wheel of suffering which is human existence in this life. The song "wheel in the sky keeps on turning", by Journey, sums it up well.

Understand that surrendering the ego and its attachments will free you from unnecessary anxiety and allow your energy to flow more freely. This is the state of self-realization or Moksha. You become the Seer not the scene. In fact, the word Rishi means Seer. A good metaphor for this relationship is Radha Krishna. It is a famous piece of art from ancient times depicting Krishna playing a flute and Radha dancing. Without the flute player there is no dance.

A simple way of understanding the path of the Rishi is a statement by Krishna "you are entitled to act but not to the fruits of your actions."

The Bible also states, Adam and Eve ate the forbidden fruit and were cast out from Eden or a free communion with the cosmic force due to selfishness. What this means is we need to remain connected with the Universe, have a purpose, and must pursue a life of righteous action aimed at helping others with whatever dilemma is placed in front of us.

Much mental suffering comes from wanting to get credit or attention or the lack thereof. After we have done something, we expect something back. I tell many of my corporate clients just focus on helping the organization and your team will succeed. Everything is related to providing your talent in a selfless manner and timing which is determined by planetary movements. Influence is under your control but not the end outcome. We must also lead from the heart with truth, for it will indeed set you free from the bondage of your mind.

This brings me back to Vedic Astrology which I have already discussed. All Rishis were schooled in Astrological Sciences as part of Yoga. It is the science of light and planets.

In the Brihat Hora Shastra, the book of Vedic astrology written by Maha Rishi Parashara, he states "Spirit is unbounded Consciousness", the universal Soul or Self is identified with Vishnu. The observer in you is the bit of super soul animating you and me. All beings have their own ego individuality as well as Spirit. Some beings have more individuality, and some are more spirit. The Sun and the planets are not just big rocks in the sky they are primarily spiritual forces. Maharishi Parashara states, God manifested the planets so that we could experience the fruits of our Karmas. The earth and planets came from the Sun and we came from the earth and elements. The electromagnetic forces they generate influence life on earth.

When we are born, we emit a frequency based on the time and place of our birth which attracts a physical and emotional life around it. This is affected by the movement of the planets. Our physical body and mental experiences are bound to the slings and arrows of outrageous fortune, as Shakespeare pointed out in Hamlet. However, by self-effort we can connect back to unbounded Consciousness, and enter the cosmic flow, relieving ourselves from much suffering. This is the path of the eternal way. In short, you get in touch with your intuition which transcends the grip of your mind.

A NEW VISION

It is vital that we keep a healthy body by exercising regularly, eating a balanced diet, and avoiding excess indulgence in refined foods and intoxicants. Then we should follow a disciplined life, focused on being helpful and courageously confronting and transcending our own ego. We must also protect the less fortunate, and the animals of this earth as they were here first. The main things we have to learn how to deal with as humans are transcending anger, lust, greed, possessiveness, and fear. This aligns us with the positive frequency of the electromagnetic grid of the cosmos and has an uplifting effect.

The way to do this is abandoning all support and being emotionally self-reliant. Align with your higher mind and trust in Consciousness to guide you. Examine your life. You will see whatever you have to experience in your life you will go through. How you handle it is up to you and alters your destiny. Nothing is left out. Letting go of fear and trusting the universe by abandoning selfish motives is the key to the path of the Rishi. As you get better at this level of thought, your perceived suffering will be much less.

I have had the opportunity to know many well-meaning Yoga instructors here in America. The funny thing is beyond saying Namaste and knowing all sorts of physical Yoga poses, or Asanas, many are unschooled in Yoga philosophy. Asanas or yoga poses are definitely helpful in connecting your mind with your body and helping you becoming more flexible, but are a minor aspect of the science of Yoga.

Mainstream Yoga is being commercialized into things like hot yoga, gymnastic yoga, and goat yoga. An entire industry of expensive Yoga pants costing hundreds of dollars has developed. Take for example the athleisure marketing movement catering to this segment; It is worth billions.

Hatha Yoga and Surya Namaskar are a series of exercises worshiping the Sun. They were developed by Rishis of old to straighten the spine to allow for good posture. This is because meditation requires you to sit upright and be still, so the chakras get aligned with the help of specific breathing techniques. With upright meditation one is better able to go inside the mind and perceive the self. Physical Yoga has no other purpose.

To understand the science of Yoga or unifying with Universal energy, it is important to read and comprehend and reflect upon the authentic sources.

Samkhya Philosophy of Maharishi Kapila, The Bhagavad Gita, Yoga Vasishta, The Upanishads, Yoga Sutras of Patanjali, The Crest Crown jewel of Discrimination by Adi Shankara, and Rig Veda are the main manuscripts of Yoga contemplation and study. It is only by integrating these teachings and internalizing them that one becomes self-aware. Any serious student of Yoga should read these books as they are the foundation of Yoga practice. All other Yoga is an offshoot.

Yoga is a way of uniting with Consciousness and is not a religion. Even a little Yoga practice will make you more peaceful. There is also a logical and scientific basis to it.

Each person has a different body, and as we journey through life, we experience many different things. Nevertheless, a balanced mind and self-awareness will allow for the most optimal experience.

THE COSMIC SCIENCE OF BEING

The main scientific thing to realize is that the milky way galaxy rotates around a galactic center. Light and electromagnetic frequency emanates from there. The Sun in our solar system was formed about 5 billion years ago, from particles of space dust and dust collapsing on itself due to gravity. Once the Sun formed the remaining gas and dust around the Sun began to coalesce and became the planets which all fell in to orbit around the sun.

The earth formed as one of these planets followed by the Moon. The Moon and its orbit around the earth created the atmosphere. Life exploded during the Cambrian period around 500 million years ago, when the Moon entered the earth's orbit and stabilized the atmosphere.

Our bodies are a product of the earth elements and water. Why is it so hard to believe that our physical bodies are related to the Sun, Moon and planets? We are star stuff infused by Consciousness which animates us and gives us life, as Carl Sagan would say. However, many people are more inclined to believe in Santa Clause than Astrology.

The whole aim of life according to the Rishis is to transcend our gross physical form and align with Universal Consciousness, thus detaching our preoccupation and pure identification with the physical experience which is the source of misery. In short, life is living us and we are reacting.

As the planets move, we are affected based on our physical make up and time of birth. They trigger events in our lives so we can grow and evolve. The sole purpose of life is to evolve and connect with cosmic light, and realize it is a multiverse out there and our human body is but one element of it.

Contracting from life by being self-serving is being body bound, ego enslaved, and Karmically bound to ideas of me and mine. This kind of us and them thinking is the root cause of mental agitation and disturbance. We are all like Salmon swimming upstream and trying to find our source of being. However, we are not Salmon, we are beings with much greater intelligence. The more we elevate our mind the more we perceive and the less selfish we become. We cannot change the whole world, but we can change ourselves and influence the thinking of those we come into contact with.

PRACTICAL APPLICATION
OF RISHI THINKING

Entering into the way of a Rishi requires two things, Sadhana, or practice of dedicated focused meditation, and Tapasaya, or sacrifice of the ego through discipline of body mind and speech. This can be achieved in a variety of ways. Maha Rishi Patanjali discusses this in the Yoga Sutras as Yama's or a moral code of conduct and Niyama's observances practice and behavior. This prepares you for higher states of union with Consciousness.

Yama or Right Living Practices

1. Do no harm to other living beings
2. Tell the truth; it sets you free
3. Non-Stealing and non-possessiveness
4. Regulation and moderation of sexual energy or life force
5. Non-hoarding and avoidance of greed

Niyama's or Behaviors

1. Keep yourself clean at all times
2. Practice contentment
3. Develop self-discipline and focus
4. Practice self-study and self-analysis
5. Surrender your ego to the universal life force

Vedic science postulates the wheel life is divided into four areas: Dharma which is duty and responsibility, Artha wealth and the pursuit of it, Kama physical enjoyment and pleasure, and Moksha liberation or spiritual enlightenment. Each area of life lived in harmony with cosmic forces brings peace and satisfaction. When we are out of balance it can create suffering. I will discuss this in detail later. Our urge to live is dictated by Prakriti or nature which consists of Tamas, Rajas, and Sattva. Each individual is a mix of these in different combinations.

The three can be equated to the three states of matter solid, liquid and gas. The Tamasic state is when a person reflects very little cosmic light and is body bound, ignorant, and selfishly living life for nothing but sense enjoyment. Greed, compulsiveness and selfishness predominate. Rajas is when a person is active, engaged, and competitive, living life with purpose but subject to emotional up and downs and anger. The connection to others is evident. Sattva is harmony, balance, and a sense of connectedness with others. The impulse to connect with something greater than our ego is present and gentleness and compassion is evident.

GODS AND DEMONS

Rishi thinking articulates there are god like forces and demonic forces that interplay within each of us. The god like forces are called Devas and are Sattvic, uplifting, and evolving human beings into pure bliss Consciousness. The Demonic forces are described as Assura's and are Tamasic anti-evolutionary and want to exist in the material, resisting change and preventing evolution. These are the forces of Artha and Kama representing: materialism, lust, greed, power, ambition, and conspicuous consumption. This is why all of us struggle between doing the right thing and being self-serving and self-indulgent.

These forces are natural, and it is through the effort of discipline and consistent practice that we transcend and evolve the human condition into a spiritual being, capable of perceiving a multiverse of many dimensions.

Most of us over the age of 40 have a similar field of experience that is quite common irrespective of gender, race, or financial condition. We are born to experience sense enjoyment like eating, drinking, sex. We aspire for wealth, status and recognition. Along the way, we have many moments of joy experience being loved and giving love. Most of us have many successful moments. However, it is also true that we are subject to aging, loss, betrayal, and disease. Nothing it seems lasts forever. After experiencing sufficient disappointment in life, we turn inwards to find meaning. Meditation is a great way to achieve this.

I was fortunate enough to have attended a speech by Maharishi Mahesh Yogi who brought Vedic thinking, Transcendental

Meditation, Vedic Astrology, and Ayurveda to the west. I myself was initiated into Transcendental Meditation and given a mantra that settles the mind, and allows for more relaxation and evolution of the higher mind. I found that the people teaching Transcendental mantra meditation were technicians, taught the technical aspects of teaching the process. None of them seemed particularly enlightened. However, this is a great foundation for beginning meditation.

 My more in-depth studies revealed these are seed mantras from Tantric Yoga. Shakti mantras are ways to connect to the Divine mother who controls creative energy. They are also known as seed mantras. The main ones are: OM, Aim, Hrim, Krim, Hum, Strim, Aim, Shrim, Klim, Hlim. The idea is to turn the mind inward towards a more Sattvic vibration. Or, as Maharishi says connecting with pure bliss cosmic intelligence to settle the mind.

These seed mantras help us overcome our Asura side and rest in a higher Deva state. It is fair to say God is in you. However, the trick is to connect with this higher frequency and allow divine grace to enter into matter. The more sattvic you are the more you reflect divine light. The more Tamasic, the less you reflect light and are focused more on sense gratification.

Through a program of focused meditation and pranayama, or breath control, it is possible to allow the mind to enter a state of infinite Consciousness and perceive the sound Aum. The primal humming sound antecedent to all other thoughts. In the Bible, it states in the beginning there was the word and Jesus stated "the Kingdom of heaven is in you."

The idea is by this sacrifice and discipline we uplift ourselves from being attached to the body mind complex. By doing so, we achieve liberation from bondage to flesh and all that is associated with it.

It took me over five years of consistent meditation and discipline to achieve twenty minutes of this state, on a daily basis. The immediate benefit is that the mind begins to realize how tight and stressed the body is and relieving the tension in the body becomes easy. The second level one gets from meditation is that once you come out of this state you perceive things differently. Most notably you begin to be more at ease at letting go of circumstances you don't control. The final stage is a state of observing your thoughts as they arise spontaneously, and not getting caught up in the freight train of your own mind. All of this puts one in a relaxed peaceful easeful state.

When one is peaceful and easeful there is no longer any need to impress others, or seek to fit in, or be accepted by anyone except yourself. This is the biggest benefit of the Rishi perception. Complete self-acceptance and a state of non-agitation. People pay thousands of dollars to therapists to achieve this state, but it can be done for free at your home, and by yourself, if you understand and follow the way of the eternal way. This does require self-effort and commitment.

STEPS TO LIBERATION FROM SELF TYRANNY

The Rishi way is aimed at freeing us from our self-imposed suffering. I will now discuss how to navigate this path. There many happy moments in life, such as eating good food, getting a good job, falling in love, experiencing joy and acquiring material objects that signify wealth and status. There is a lot of suffering as well.

As I expressed earlier, most of us will experience many losses before we are prepared to look inward. Betrayal from close friends, job losses, family drama, disease, humiliation, separation and death are all part of the spectrum of difficult experiences we all go through in life.

If indeed we are all going to go through this sequence at some point, what is the purpose of living? The answer is to unite with or experience union or Yoga with eternal being. This is not to say your problems will vanish. Nevertheless, by doing so it will allow you to experience more peace of mind and less suffering, as you go through your Karmic experience.

The twelve houses on your Vedic birth chart, each relate to a different area of life known as Purusharthas, or aims of life. First house is a Dharma house, Second Artha, third Kama, and fourth Moksha. This sequence repeats itself three times, for a total of all twelve houses. I will unpack more about this concept in the next chapter.

A close look at each of these areas unfolds a lot about the personality. The placement of the Sun, Moon, Venus, Jupiter, Saturn Mars, and Mercury, as well as the nodes Rahu and Ketu, and ruling planet of the Ascendant will show which areas of life are going to be the focus in this lifetime.

More than three planets in one house of the birth chart shows this area of life as very important. Some people have more lessons to learn by pursuing righteousness, some wealth, others physical pleasure, and some spiritual liberation. Each of us came for a Karmic reason.

A trained Vedic Astrologer with a Spiritual focus, such as myself, can easily view your Karmic pattern from your birth chart. I have incorporated this science into Life Coaching and have had significant success in helping people understand themselves better.

THE CHAKRAS AND THEIR RELATIONSHIP TO PLANETS

Each planet activates different energy centers or chakras in our nervous system which is energized through Prana or breath.

1. The first chakra is known as Muladhara and is connected to Saturn. It is located at the base of the tailbone. It is related to grounding or security.
2. The second chakra is known as Svadhisthana and is connected to Jupiter. It is located in the sex organs. This chakra is related to expansion and enjoyment.
3. The third chakra is known as Manipura and is connected to Mars. It is located in the solar plexus and is where our vital force resides.
4. The fourth chakra is known as Anahata and is connected to Venus. It is located in the heart. It relates to our capacity to love and be loved.
5. The fifth chakra is known as Vishuddhi and is connected to Mercury. It is located in the throat area and relates to rational thought and speech.
6. The sixth chakra is known as Ajna. It is located between the eyebrows and is connected to the Moon. It is the seat of the third eye and the seat of extrasensory perception and intuition. It is the gateway to the astral world.
7. The seventh chakra is known as Sahasrara. It is located in the crown of the head and connects us to the electromagnetic energy of the Sun. It is known as the thousand

petal lotus. All other chakras have to be aligned for this to activate fully.

Balancing the chakras requires following a disciplined ethical code of conduct, by balancing the four major areas of life also known as Purusharthas, I mentioned them earlier. They are: Dharma, Artha, Kama, and Moksha. Understanding the nuances of these four areas of life is invaluable to any spiritual seeker. I will explain them in detail.

DHARMA – TAKING RESPONSIBILITY FOR YOUR LIFE CIRCUMSTANCES

We are all born with a Karmic burden to transcend. When life takes a turn in the wrong direction, it is easy to blame our parents or others. Dharma is understanding and taking responsibility for overcoming your circumstances. It is also creating an environment that is fair and equitable, through our ability to influence our circumstances using our intelligence. Dharma is the power that upholds the world and keeps the universe balanced on a cosmic level through individual right action. This is accomplished by the following steps:

1. Take full responsibility for your emotional state. It is up to you to establish a sense of equanimity and calm mindset through life's challenges. Creating drama is unnecessary.
2. You sometimes don't choose your circumstances, but you do control how you respond. Do not be emotionally pulled into other people's drama.
3. Whatever circumstance you are in, do what you can to help without seeking something in return
4. Practice non-greed and contentment by not being envious of others. Everything has a price.
5. Fight the good fight with compassion and speak the truth with diplomacy even with your own family.
6. Whatever your feelings about your family try and maintain good relations, especially with your parents by

making an effort to stay connected.
7. Be caring and supportive with your significant other. A life partner is a thought partner.

ARTHA – THE PURSUIT OF WEALTH AND ITS PROPER APPLICATION

It has been my experience that no matter how much money you have or whatever your job title, disease, disappointment, fear, and death will not escape you for long. So how do we have a proper relationship with money? I think we can all agree, it is hard to earn money, harder to keep it, and not be consumed by being obsessed by it.

As any good financial planner would tell you, the first step to having a proper relationship with money is to make a list of your needs and wants. Your needs are essential, your wants are not. The trick is to clarify your needs.

Your needs are to live a comfortable life which includes:

1. A roof over your head.
2. Money to pay your utilities.
3. Money to pay for good food.
4. Money to pay for healthcare.
5. Money to pay for clothing and transportation.
6. Caring for a pet.
7. Savings to live on when you are old and retired; Seven times your annual after-tax earnings.

The way to do this is enjoy your life till you are thirty. Indulge in all pleasure's money can buy. Just be sure you have an emergency fund equal to three months of living expenses. It is important that you enjoy and experience fun in your life. You never know when your time is up. After that save 20% of your income till you are forty.

 After forty, save 25%. Invest it wisely. Spend 25 % on your personal enjoyment and wants like vacations, eating out, and personal care. Use 50% for your essential needs, like house payments, food, clothing medical insurance, and fitness. Never live your life to impress others, it is a waste of cash. Living within your means is imperative.

Have a good accord with your significant other about living a life of minimal debt, if any. Be generous with others if you have extra to help out. In our case, we live in a neighborhood that is middle class and safe, though we could live in a more opulent fashion. However, we made the determination it is unnecessary to bling up. Instead, we live comfortably but save for a rainy day which has brought us a lot of security, knowing if something happens to our income, we have no debt, own our home, and have access to several years of financial resources to live quite well!

The top 90 percentile of self-made millionaires in America have a net worth of around 3 million dollars. They live comfortably but well below their means which is why they are millionaires. In short, they understand the value of money and have a proper relationship with it. They are secure about themselves and don't try to impress others.

Some of you might laugh when I mention a pet as essential. I am a big fan of dogs. I have found that by learning to have a proper relationship with one they are indeed man's best friend. A dog is a great personal trainer. Walking them daily gets you to exercise and get fresh air, as well as enjoy nature. Caring for an animal also puts you in a nurturing role that opens your heart. In return they give you unconditional friendship and love which places you in a good mental spot. It is a well-known fact pets can reduce your blood pressure. They live in the present and teach you not to dwell on yourself. Pets are capable of seeing, hearing and smelling at a very subtle level. They can sense your moods. Sadly, you will outlive them but that is the circle of life. Dogs have been companions to people for several thousands of years. It is well known they can smell changes in your body before a seizure and they can even smell cancer. They can also see your aura. I have always had dogs in my life and currently have a Yellow Labrador named Rebel and a Border Terrier named Ketu.

KAMA - PHYSICAL AND SENSUAL ENJOYMENT

It is vital that we appreciate that we are spiritual beings in a physical body. The body is by its nature attached to the senses touch, sight, hearing, taste, and smell. So, it makes sense we are inclined to enjoy touching and being touched. Sex is the most enjoyable touching pleasure; some indulgence in it is a beautiful thing. Sex opens up the chakras which are related to the planets, particularly Saturn the energy of restriction and Jupiter the planet of expansion. The Indian book of sexual poses, The Kama Sutra is aimed at achieving maximum physical pleasure. Though one would have to be pretty flexible and fit to participate in some of the poses. Additionally, seeing beautiful things like flowers, hearing pleasant music, eating and drinking tasty foods, or the smell of nice fragrances, open up our pleasure centers. All these are natural tendencies and should be enjoyed.

In the previous section on Artha, I mentioned till the age of 30, enjoy the physical pleasure of life as much as possible. As you age you need moderation and need to be more selective. It is ok to experience sense gratification of all kinds, so you are sated. Suppressing natural urges will only lead to a hidden life of compulsive and possibly perverse behavior. Fully enjoying your body as long as you do not violate the rights of others is perfectly normal. It is only then that most of us can begin balancing the senses. This following seven steps work.

1. Explore and enjoy your body and sexuality without guilt or shame. It is perfectly natural to enjoy sex and

think about it.

2. Exercise regularly for the body machine needs to be kept fit, so it can be enjoyed.
3. After the age of thirty, practice monogamy as it focuses you. Trust and loyalty with a significant other are key to spiritual advancement.
4. Eat a tasty balanced nutritious diet and indulge in intoxicants moderately.
5. Have fresh flowers of varied colors in your house. Listen to uplifting or calming music.
6. Utilize bodywork such as massage. It does wonders for your health.
7. Keep your body clean and use good posture when sitting or walking.

God gave you a body to experience and fully enjoy. Do so every day without guilt or harming other people. The trick is to do so in moderation.

MOKSHA – THE FINAL COUNTDOWN

Moksha is not a place or destination. It is an experience, the dissolving of individual differentiation into super-conscious. Whether it is Buddha talking about Nirvana by following Noble truths, or Maharishi Kapila explaining Purusha and Prakriti, the ultimate goal of life is to achieve a calm and balanced state of mind free from fear and anxiety. This is described as Satchidananda or pure bliss Consciousness. Shankaracharya describes, it is freeing oneself in this life from the illusions of the mind or Maya.

We are born with a Karmic blueprint that has a bell-shaped curve of possibilities, based on our choices. If I were to put a percentage on it, I would say most people, 80% fall in the center and have ups and downs. 10% suffer a lot on the far end of the curve due to wrong choices, and 10% achieve a state of Moksha due to right thinking and choices.

It goes without saying, some people experience more challenges and obstacle in their lives than others. This is due to samskaras or mental tendencies of this life and previous lives working their way out. However, the more closely we are aligned with cosmic forces and the universal laws the less we suffer. Tools such as Vedic Astrology, Meditation, and right code of conduct show you the way.

Here are some specific steps to place you on the road to liberation in this lifetime. Most of it comes from Yoga and is the underlying theme of all Yoga. It originates from the Sanskrit term of "Yug" or unite with the Universal Consciousness.

However, no one is ready to achieve the road of Moksha till they have had enough of life and its dramatics. This is why I explained till the age of thirty people should enjoy their lives for the most part, and seek every experience they want without guilt as long as you do not harm others. Follow the golden rule of Jesus. "Do on to others as you would have them do unto you"

The seven steps to Moksha

1. The first step to freedom is understanding there is a Physical reality, but how we feel about it is an optical and perceptual illusion of the mind, based on beliefs and attachment. This is Maya or illusion.
2. The human body has essential needs: food, family, fitness, nature, and safe place to sleep. All other needs are wants and not necessary.
3. We are responsible for maintaining a healthy body through exercise, eating good food, and spending time in nature.
4. All urges we feel are natural and should be allowed to express themselves, without harming others. We are all subject to Karma and we need to transcend above animal nature.
5. Aligning yourself with the cosmic forces through right behavior. Meditation is the practical way of transcending your body and mind.
6. Recognize you are a solidified piece of Consciousness and so are others. The ultimate reality is that we are spirit, and when we die, we are absorbed back into super-consciousness.
7. Following a life aligned with natural law, or Sanatana Dharma, to unite you with supreme Consciousness is the aim of life. Acknowledging you are connected to all

beings enables this.

Letting go of fear, anger, possessiveness and the need to impress others with shiny objects leads to a life of freedom. Using the tools of Vedic astrology and meditation will show you the way.

SECRET OF SOLAR MEDITATION

The Brihadaranyaka or Forest Upanishad is one of the Principal Upanishads. It is attributed to Maharishi Yajnavalkya. He has an interesting story. He was an excellent student and meditator who eventually became advisor to the King. His journey was not easy. He fell out of favor of his Guru because he was not traditional and a bit too smart for his teacher's liking. His teacher asked Yajnavalkya to give back all the knowledge of Vedas which he had gained from him. Being an obedient student, upon the Guru's order, Yajnavalkya gave back the knowledge and left the Ashram.

Being disturbed by his Guru's treatment, Yajnavalkya decided not to approach any human guru for learning again. Instead, he performed meditation to the Sun God Surya, and asked him to bless him with eternal knowledge. Lord Surya became happy with Yajnavalkya's devotion and bestowed him with supreme wisdom. Once again, the Sun is the visible form of divine light on the planet and should be contemplated on.

I have tried all sorts of meditation, but meditation to the Sun is simple and focused and can help you rapidly advance. The most important and one of the oldest mantras is the Gayatri mantra which is a prayer to the Sun, and it appears in the Rig Veda.

"Om bhur bhuvah svah tat savitur varenyam bhargo devasya dhimahi dhiyo

yo nah prachodayat". Translated from Sanskrit it means:

Om, the cause of everything, the earth, the space in between and the worlds above. That Solar being is the one who is the most worshipful. We invoke that shining, all knowing being. May that being set our minds in the right direction.

PREPARING TO MEDITATE

Meditation cannot just be entered into. That is why most people cannot remain still and quiet for even five minutes. It requires some pre-work. This consists of being mindful of your posture when you stand, sit, and eat. An erect spine is important. Secondly, doing a mental body scan of which areas of your body are tense, in the morning, noon, and evening. Focus on relaxing those areas through breathing and gentle stretching. Third, learn to connect with people by looking them in the eye, and inquiring why do I get tense around certain people.

By doing all these things you reduce your contraction from life and you begin to relax. Remember, Consciousness is flowing through you; allow it to flow without blocking the energy.

CLEARING YOUR BREATH
OR PRANA

Before you begin to meditate, clear your breathing channels by practicing alternate nostril breathing. Breath or Prana is life. It sustains the body not only through the lungs but also nerve channels.

The human body contains 72,000 nerve points that channel vital breath to every cell. When this system flows freely, we are healthy; when it becomes weak, we struggle with mental agitation which also affects physical health.

There are 3 main channels that transmit energy. The Sushumna nadi is the body's main channel, running from the base of the spine to the crown of the head, passing through each of the seven chakras in its course. It is the channel through which Kundalini *Shakti* or the bodies electromagnetic energy rises. This awakening process connects with higher spiritual consciousness. It connects the Muladhara (root) chakra, to its true home, at the Sahasrara chakra at the crown of the head. The Sushumna nadi is the central path to the energy of the Cosmos. The Ida nadi begins and ends on the left side of Sushumna. Ida is regarded as the Lunar nadi, cool and nurturing by nature, and is said to control all mental processes. Pingala, the Solar nadi, begins and ends to the right of Sushumna. It is warm and stimulating by nature, controls all vital physical processes. The interaction between Ida and Pingala corresponds to the internal dance between intuition and rationality, male and female, the right and left-brain hemispheres. Bringing Ida and Pingala into equilibrium is a major focus of meditation.

The most powerful method of balancing breath is alternate nostril breathing. A few rounds of this basic breathing technique, at the beginning of meditation, is an excellent way to help restore equilibrium between the two channels

To practice alternate nostril breathing, sit in a comfortable meditative position. Close the left nostril with a finger and inhale fully through the right, close it with a finger, release the left nostril, and exhale through it. Inhale through the left nostril, close it with a finger, release the right nostril, and exhale through it. This completes one round. Do seven rounds. This helps with creating physical and emotional equilibrium, clearing the way for your meditative practice spiritual growth.

MEDITATION - THE INNER PORTAL TO THE UNIVERSE

Here are ten practical steps to solar meditation. If you have a quiet place outside in nature where you can do this, that is preferable, otherwise dedicate a room in your house that faces east for your Meditation practice. The important thing about meditation is not to force anything. It should be a gradual process of relaxing and integrating the body mind with the cosmic flow.

Steps to Meditation

1. Begin your practice on Sunday which is the Solar day according to Vedic Astrology.
2. Arrange for a clean room with a window facing east where the Sun rises.
3. Awake at dawn, clean your body, drink a glass of pure water.
4. Arrange for a comfortable chair facing the rising Sun and sit, keeping your spine straight and body relaxed.
5. Mentally find three things in your life that you are grateful for and give thanks.
6. Scan your body and relax any tension, feel the rays of the Sun, and feel the warmth. Do seven rounds of alternate nostril breathing.
7. Exhale completely. Then, inhale and mentally

> chant the Gayatri Mantra while holding a mental image of the Sun.
>
> 8. Slowly inhale directing the breath to the base of your spine; exhale the breath focusing on the center of your forehead, the Ajna Chakra.
> 9. Continue to breathe in and out slowly approximately ten seconds each way, 108 times.
> 10. Observe your thoughts and breathe through any negative feelings.

Change your focus from gripping things to letting go. At first, start with five minutes every morning. Over a period of several months, increase the time you meditate to twenty minutes or thirty minutes. It is not practical for most people to do more, neither is it necessary to get the benefits. The quality and depth of your meditation is more important than the time you spend doing it. What is important is you do this on a regular basis.

In the first few weeks, it is not uncommon to have disturbing thoughts arise from your past while you attempt to meditate. This is your body's way of releasing toxic energy. What is important is that you breathe through these thoughts and release the tension around them.

Why 108 breaths? It is a sacred number in advanced Yoga practice. The diameter of the Sun is about 108 times of the diameter of Earth. The distance between the Earth and the Sun is approximately 108 times the Sun's diameter. The distance between the Earth and Moon is 108 times the diameter of the Moon. There is a magical frequency to this number.

It was difficult for me at first, but now I can enter a meditative state quickly and maintain it for twenty minutes every morning. A calm state of being saturates my being and I am able to deal with the challenges of life in a non-reactive fashion.

The biggest benefit of meditation is understanding that you are the origin of your thoughts. Most fearful thoughts subside and dissolve once you observe them rather than react. You become the thermostat of your being. As a consequence, you enter into a peaceful balanced state of mind which translates to the rest of your day; less stress, anxiety, lower blood pressure, and better sleep are also a benefit. Always keep in mind, no matter what happens in your life you will be ok.

CONCLUSION

I wrote this book as a self-help book, to help you come to terms with the fact that you are responsible for your emotional state and the choices you make in your life. Our mind is a prism reflecting thought. Planets are a manifestation of Universal life force and our lives are heavily influenced by them. We are part of a cosmic matrix and our awareness is part of a multiverse with many dimensions. Ancient knowledge points out, through discipline, self-awareness, and correct lifestyle, we can align with cosmic forces, transcend our mental tendencies and have a much better quality of life. Freedom from self-tyranny and dependence on others for our peace of mind is freedom. Namaste!

Bibliography

1. Aryan Invasion Theory, Stephen Knapp: The Final Nail in the Coffin, Amazon Kindle Edition, Amazon 2012
2. Astrology of the Seers, David Frawley, WI: Lotus Press, 2000
3. Beneath the Vedic Sky: Introduction to The Astrology of Ancient

India, William Levacy, CA: Hay House, 1999

4. Brihat Parashara Hora Shastra, Maharishi Parasara, New Delhi: Sagar Publications 1994

5. Easy Death, Spiritual Wisdom on the Ultimate Transcending of Death and Everything Else, Adi DA Samraj CA, Dawn Horse Press, CA, 1991

6. Graha Sutras, Ernst Wilhelm, Kala Occult Publishers, CA, 2016

7. History of the First Council of Nicea, Dean Dudely, Biblio Life LLC 2009

8. The Lost Continent of Kumari Kandam, Sudeep S Amazon Kindle Edition, Amazon 2020

9. Mahabaratha, The Greatest Spiritual Epic of All Time, New Delhi: Indra Printers, 2000

10. Primer of Tamil Literature, M.S Purnalingam Pillai, Madras, Ananda Press, 1904

11. Pythagoras and The Early Pythagoreans, Lenoid Zhmud, Oxford University Press, UK 2012

12. Rigveda the earliest Poetry of India, Veda Vayas, Translated by Stephanie. W Jamison and Joel P Brereton, Oxford University Press, NY Branch, 2014

13. Shankaras Crest Crown Jewel of Discrimination, Swami Prhabivananda, Vedanta Society, CA, 1975

14. Yoga Sutras of Patanjali, Swami Satchidananda Integral Yoga Publications, VA, Revised Edition 2012

15. Vasishta's Yoga, Swami Venkatesananda, Divine Life Society, State University of New York Press, 1993

16. Vishnu Purina, Translated by H.H Wilson, Oxford University, 1840, Kindle Edition, Eventy Publishing Inc, 2009

ABOUT THE AUTHOR

Cyril Joseph Neicheril

He is a Life Coach and Vedic Astrologer who lives in Portland, Oregon. He is an expert in the field of Yoga Philosophy, and has been a Yoga practitioner for over twenty years.
You may contact him at www.vedicfit.net